Rejoice!
It's Christmas

Carol Fears

MOORLEY'S Print & Publishing

British Library Cataloguing in Publication Data.
A catalogue record for this book is available
from the British Library.

Cover illustration: Greg Clifton

ISBN 0 86071 557 4

MOORLEY'S Print & Publishing
23 Park Rd., Ilkeston, Derbys DE7 5DA
Tel/Fax: (0115) 932 0643

Contents

MOORLEY'S

We are growing publishers, adding several new titles to our list each year. We also undertake private publications and commissioned works.

Our range of publications includes:

Books of Verse:
Devotional Poetry
Recitations
Drama
Bible Plays
Sketches
Nativity Plays
Passiontide Plays
Easter Plays
Demonstrations
Resource Books
Assembly Material
Songs and Musicals
Children's Addresses
Prayers and Graces
Daily Readings
Books for Speakers
Activity Books
Quizzes
Puzzles
Painting Books
Church Stationery
Notice Books
Cradle Rolls
Hymn Board Numbers

Please send a stamped addressed envelope (approx. 9" x 6") for the current catalogue or consult your local Christian Bookshop who should stock or be able to order our titles.

THE STAR OF CHRISTMAS

There were shepherds on the hillside,
There was an angel train,
And a bright new constellation,
The night when Jesus came.

A little inn at Bethlehem
With not a room to spare,
There was Mary, there was Joseph,
To keep Him in their care.

An empty manger cradled Him,
And shepherds came to see
The Son of God Incarnate,
Who was born for you and me.

That was a long, long time ago
That love was sent to earth,
Yet every year we celebrate
The day of Jesus' birth.

As we look back through the years,
Do we look forward too?
To Jesus coming in the clouds
To call for me and you.

A trumpet will be blown next time,
And Jesus will be King;
He will shine forth and be the star,
And our new song we'll sing.

THE ANGELS' SONG

Praise to God in the highest,
And on earth goodwill to men,
It is peace we bring,
That is why we sing,
Jesus came to Bethlehem.

(Suggested tune: I am H.A.P.P.Y.)

CHRISTMAS

In Bethlehem's inn there was no room
When God's Son Jesus came to earth,
Our first visitor 'out of this world'
Was offered a manger for His birth.

Each year December the twenty fifth,
A date remembered above all other,
A great big birthday party is held,
And people give gifts to one another.

Do you realise Jesus is alive?
He watches as every year does pass,
It is His birthday we celebrate;
Is Christ a part of your Christmas?

This year why not worship Him for once,
And welcome Him as you would a friend,
Give Him the gift of your life and love,
And you will know Christmas without end!

THE MESSAGE OF CHRISTMAS

On Christmas Day God sent His Son,
The Prince of Peace for everyone;
He came to earth goodwill to bring,
The message that God's choir did sing.

A precious gift, God's only Son,
Sent to bring peace to everyone;
He was God's gift, He was not lent,
To every tribe and nation sent.

Then why do all the nations war?
Where is the peace they're looking for?
Peace came to earth and he was slain,
Did God send Jesus Christ in vain?

No! Jesus will come back again,
The Prince of Peace will come to reign;
He offers life and peace to all
Who at His feet will humbly fall.

This Christmas let CHRIST be a part,
Let Jesus be born in your heart,
He is the Way, the Truth, the Life,
The Prince of Peace and end of strife.

If all the world would claim Him King,
Goodwill to all men He would bring,
If all the nations to Him bow,
We could have peace on earth right now.

THE WISE MEN

In our Bible we are told
How wise men, sages of old,
Followed Jesus' natal star
Across the desert, travelling far.

They stopped off at Jerusalem,
Where King Herod summoned them,
To bring him word of Jesus' home,
So he to worship Him could come.

The star led to Bethlehem,
Over the house that sheltered Him,
The wise men gave gifts that were
Gold and frankincense and myrrh.

They rejoiced with greatest joy
When they saw the little boy,
And fell down and worshipped Him
Who they knew was born a King.

God warned them Herod to ignore,
So they went to him no more,
Travelling back another way,
As Herod schemed Jesus to slay.

But God protected His blest Son,
He told Joseph to quickly run
Into Egypt, with Jesus and Mary;
Joseph obeyed, he did not tarry.

Herod sent his men and slew
Every child to the age of two,
Jesus that age could have been
Since His natal star was seen.

NATIVITY HYMN
(Suggested tune 'Puff the Magic Dragon')

Jesus came to Israel
Long, long ago,
Was cradled in a manger,
The love of God to show.

Refrain: Just a tiny baby,
Born in a stall,
So many, many years ago,
And yet He loves us all.

Angels came to shepherds,
Good news to bring,
"Peace on earth, goodwill to men,"
The heavenly choir did sing.

Shepherds came to Jesus,
With no delay,
There they knelt and worshipped Him,
Their Saviour born today.

Wise men came to Jesus,
Led by a star,
Gifts they brought to honour Him,
Gold, frankincense and myrrh.

Won't you come to Jesus,
Why stay away?
He's knocking at your heart's door,
Open to Him today.

CHRISTMAS PRAISE

Praise to our God for His only Son,
Down to our lowly earth He has come,
Rejoice all people on this great morn,
In an old cowshed Jesus is born.

Shine out star in the east,
He is a Saviour, Prophet and Priest,
Heavenly angels come down and sing,
Welcome on earth our new born King.

Draw near shepherds kneel and adore
This is the Child that you're looking for,
You were informed by heavenly throng,
He is the theme of the angels' song.

Wise men of east who have travelled far,
Led by a new and brilliant star,
Worship and honour the new born King,
And offer the gifts that you do bring.

Come all you people and homage pay,
To our dear Saviour on Christmas Day,
No greater love will you ever find,
He is God's gift to all mankind.

NATIVITY POEM

When Jesus was born in Bethlehem
His only bed was a cattle stall,
Mary had no crib prepared for Him,
There was no maternity hospital.

No pretty layette to wrap Him in,
No pillow on which His head to lay,
He was meanly wrapped in swaddling bands,
And for blankets the Christ child had hay.

There wasn't a doctor or midwife
To care for the child and His mother,
They couldn't phone for the ambulance,
Or find a more suitable cover.

Only strangers came to visit them,
And many of those had travelled far,
A group of shepherds from the hillside,
And three wise men who followed a star.

But a star was lit that holy night,
And a heavenly choir proclaimed the birth,
When Jesus Christ was born of Mary,
And peace was promised to men on earth.

THE SHEPHERDS' ROLE

While Shepherds were guarding their sheep in the night,
They suddenly had a most terrible fright,
It had all been quite dark and quiet for so long,
When bright angels appeared and broke out in song.

They fell on their faces as scared as can be,
The light was so blinding, they each could not see;
"Fear not," said the angel, "for good news we bring,
In Bethlehem city is now born a King."

The angel then told them the rest of the news,
To help them find Jesus he gave them some clues;
When the angels had gone the shepherds arose
To discuss the matter, they all gathered close.

"Not only a King, but a Saviour is He,
Wrapped up in a manger, oh how can it be?"
"Well that is the message the angel gave me,
I'm going to search, are you coming to see?"

So the shepherds all over the hills they trekked,
And prayed that their sheep from all harm would be kept,
Safe from the wolves who were always a danger,
While they went searching for the Christ child's manger.

Soon they sighted a shabby old cattle shed,
Could this be the place that housed a royal bed?
They crept to the door, being shy and wary,
And there was Jesus with Joseph and Mary.

They worshipped the baby and when they had done,
They explained how the angel had bid them come;
Glorifying God and praising as well
They left for the village, the good news to tell.

Such a lowly birthplace for God's only Son,
And humble folk that God invited to come;
God does not change, He's still searching today
For humble hearts where Christ can stay.

THE INNKEEPER

There shall be a world taxation,
As Caesar Augustus said,
So everyone had to return
To where they were born and bred.

Joseph's family came from Bethlehem,
As descendants of David's line,
And Mary went along with him
As his fiancée at the time.

There was an inn in Bethlehem,
To his staff the innkeeper said,
"I think we may be very busy,
Hurry and make up every bed."

Some people had relations
Who would put them up he knew,
But others would be arriving,
And there could be quite a few.

Even he underestimated,
Travellers came by the score,
Every single room was taken
And still they knocked at his door.

"I am sorry," said the innkeeper,
"There is no room in the inn,
I've doubled up where 'er I can,
We are full up to the brim."

"Good gracious me," said Joseph
"What are we going to do?
My lady is very pregnant
And has started labour too."

"I've done my best," innkeeper said,
"As far as I am able,
But if you're really desperate
I'll clear you out the stable."

"Oh that will do," said Joseph,
"You really are very kind."
"No problem," said the innkeeper,
"If your lady does not mind."

That is how the King of Kings
Was born in a lowly manger,
Because a harassed innkeeper
Made room for a weary stranger.

The moral of this story,
Don't fill your home with things
Of only passing value, but
Make room for the King of Kings.

REJOICE! IT'S CHRISTMAS

Rejoice! For God has sent His Son
To live on earth - The Holy One,
Praise the Lord on this Christmastide,
And let His peace with you abide.

Rejoice! God chose a virgin mum
To incubate His holy Son,
In purity His love was sent,
For everyone the gift was meant.

Rejoice! God's will on Earth be done,
He came incarnate in His Son,
To bring us joy instead of sin,
So we to heaven can enter in.

Rejoice! The great transaction's done,
We have the victory through His Son;
God's Christmas gift - a baby boy,
Who brought us love and peace and joy!

THE CHRISTMAS ROBIN

In a Bethlehem cowshed,
In a corner, out of sight,
A little robin redbreast
Took some shelter for the night.

He used to come here often
To escape the wind and rain,
The cattle were so friendly,
And they let him share their grain.

This night though it was different,
The cattle weren't in the shed,
When a man and lady entered
And prepared themselves a bed.

As the little robin watched
The night was even stranger,
The couple produced a baby boy
And laid Him in the manger!

Throughout the night the baby slept,
A peace settled over all,
But early in the morning
Some shepherds had come to call.

They knelt beside the manger,
And talked of angels' praising,
The shepherds glorified the Lord,
It really was amazing!

The robin was so curious,
He had to have a closer look,
And he bravely left the rafters,
To settle on a shepherd's crook.

When he saw the holy baby,
Laying in a bed of hay,
He sang the first carol for Jesus
At the break of Christmas Day.

THE SACRIFICIAL LAMB OF GOD

In the beginning it was God's plan
That He would walk on earth with man;
But the sinful path that man has trod
Is not compatible with a holy God.

The sacrificial price for sin
Was a spotless lamb to bring to Him;
Man's sin was recurring every day,
So God sent prophets to show the way.

Man killed His prophets one by one,
And in the end God sent His Son;
The Son of God was born, and stranger,
As Lamb of God placed in a manger.

And was it not by God's design
That shepherds visited the child divine?
When John the Baptist Jesus espied,
"Behold the Lamb of God!" he cried.

God sent Jesus to pay the price,
He had to die as our sacrifice;
Jesus was born as God's Lamb on earth,
He lived a sinless life from birth.

Man nailed Him to a cross to die,
He arose as Shepherd to you and I;
Now with our Shepherd we walk where he trod,
And He leads us on to walk with God.

HAPPY BIRTHDAY JESUS

Happy birthday Jesus,
You are our toast today;
Welcome to our service,
Be near us all we pray.
We have no angel choirs,
Or stars in bright array,
No shepherds, kings with presents,
No manger strewn with hay.
But we all love you Jesus.
And need you ever near,
So bless us as we celebrate
Your birthday Jesus dear.

EMMANUEL - GOD WITH US

For God so loved the world
He sent His only Son,
Filled with His Spirit down to earth,
Emmanuel has come!

This was God's holy plan,
For God with man to dwell;
He came as Mary's baby boy,
Jesus our Emmanuel.

He left Heaven's splendid heights,
For Bethlehem's stable bare;
God's Son took the form of man,
In love beyond compare.

And God still loves the world,
He knows our every need,
And fills us with His Spirit,
God is with us indeed.

A CHILD IS BORN IN BETHLEHEM

A child is born in Bethlehem,
And angels bring the news
To shepherds watching o'er their flocks,
Such humble folk to choose.

A child is born in Bethlehem,
A bright new star appears
To lead wise men to see a King,
Long promised down the years.

A child is born in Bethlehem,
And in a manger laid
The Son of God incarnate, sent
To a young virgin maid.

A child was born in Bethlehem
Two thousand years ago,
And we have Christmas every year
Because God loves us so.

GOD'S RECIPE FOR MANKIND

Take some shepherds from a hillside,
And some wise men from afar,
A stable bare in Bethlehem,
And a bright and shining star;
Take a loving boy and maiden,
And a very wicked king,
The crying of a new born babe,
And a heavenly choir to sing;
Then God performs a miracle,
And there in a manger curled
Amongst the straw and debris lies
Jesus, Saviour of the world!

CHRISTMASTIME

Carol singers come a calling,
Holly everywhere,
Red and green the decorations,
Illuminations
Shine from windows festooned with care;
Telephones, cards, calendars send
Messages around the earth,
All combine to tell us of our
Saviour's wondrous birth.

STAR OF THE EAST

Just a little twinkling star,
Shining on a dark, still night,
Over a field in Bethlehem,
Giving some shepherds a little light.

Millions of other stars were
Lighting up the dark night sky,
Some had been around for years,
All twinkled as the earth went by.

Suddenly, a light so bright,
An angel's light did appear,
Voices and choirs filled the sky,
The little twinkles disappeared.

A message to men on earth,
God had blessed them with a King,
The shepherds fell to the ground,
As choirs of angels did sing.

The angels went, the shepherds rose,
To find the King without delay;
The night was dark again by now, so
Shining stars showed them the way.

Just a little twinkling star,
Star of the East it became,
Leading wise men to the child King,
A little star of Bible fame.

If a little star can work
Miles up there in the night sky,
By giving his best for Jesus,
How God could use you and I.

We can bring light in darkness,
Lead others to Jesus the King,
God can use us for His glory,
Then with His angels we'll sing.

WHEN JESUS CAME TO LIVE WITH MEN

When Jesus came to live with men,
Life was not easy even then,
Because Mary and Joseph had taxes to pay,
Jesus was born in a stable of hay.

When Jesus came to live with men,
Children's lives were at risk even then,
Because Herod threatened Jesus' life
Joseph fled to Egypt with his wife.

When Jesus came to live with men,
People starved in the desert even then,
For forty days Jesus did not eat,
But he had power temptation to beat.

When Jesus came to live with men,
People were lonely and homeless then,
Jesus had no wife, children or home,
And even His tomb was not His own.

When Jesus came to live with men,
There was violence and crime even then,
Jesus loved, healed and cared in the strife,
And in the end He gave His life.

Jesus, in our life there is nothing new
That you yourself have not been through;
Return O King, make all things new,
And then let mankind live with you.